Belongs to Myrna Hull

A Visual Catechism
of the Orthodox Church

Original title: Epoptiki Katixisi

Original ©: Metropolitan of Nafpaktos Hierotheos

Translated by Esther Williams

Cover art: Yannis Yeremtzes

Published by: Birth of the Theotokos Monastery
P.O Box 107, GR-321 00 Levadia-Hellas
Tel. & Fax: (0268) 31204
http://www.pelagia.org
e-mail: pelagia@pelagia.org

First edition 1999

ISBN 960-7070-42-9

Metropolitan of Nafpaktos
Hierotheos

A Visual Catechism
of the Orthodox Church

illustrated by

Yannis Yeremtzes

Birth of the Theotokos Monastery

To those for whom

Orthodoxy

is life,

image and word

Contents

The Creed

I believe in one God, the Father Almighty, Maker of heaven and earth, and of all things visible and invisible.

And in one Lord Jesus Christ, the only-begotten Son of God, begotten of the Father before all ages.

Light of Light, very God of very God, begotten, not made, consubstantial with the Father, and by whom all things were made.

Who for us men and for our salvation came down from Heaven, and was incarnate by the Holy Spirit and the Virgin Mary, and was made man.

And was crucified for us under Pontius Pilate, and suffered, and was buried.

And He rose again on the third day according to the Scriptures.

And ascended into Heaven, and sits at the right hand of the Father.

And He will come again with glory to judge the living and the dead, and His kingdom will have no end.

And in the Holy Spirit, the Lord, the Giver of Life, Who proceeds from the Father, Who with the Father and the Son together is worshipped and glorified, Who spoke by the Prophets.

And in One, Holy, Catholic and Apostolic Church.

I acknowledge one Baptism for the remission of sins.

I look for the resurrection of the dead.

And the life of the world to come. Amen.

Introduction

At times I have noticed that there are Christians who do not know the basic truths of the orthodox faith, or they confuse them with other philosophical and religious beliefs which have been prevalent in the past and are still prevalent today.

Furthermore a catechism is needed both for small children and for those men and women who come to the church to be baptised and become Orthodox Christians.

There are indeed many contemporary books which answer this purpose. Not long ago, by the Grace of God, I published such a book, which describes the way of the catechism, its method and content.

Nevertheless I think that it will be helpful to have a publication on this subject entitled «Visual Catechism» intended for small children, for those coming to be baptised, and for those adults whom it may help to consolidate what they know.

In the first part there is a visual initiation into the basic truths of our faith. The illustrations, made by the hagiographer Yannis Yeremtzes, to whom I give my thanks, are a help to a better understanding of these great truths. The short title for each illustration gives the central thought of that particular truth.

The second part gives a fuller analysis of each particular truth, but always in the form of a summary. This is mainly to help the catechist or the adult to analyse in greater detail the picture to which it refers. Of course the brief notes will stimulate the person who takes up this work to analyse further both the picture and the particular truth, making use of passages from Bible and the patristic teachings.

I hope that this work too will help us to understand the great value of being a member of the Church and of being a living Christian, united with Christ, Who is the head of the Church.

Written on the 14th of March, 1994, the first Monday of Lent, the period of the Catechism

Archimandrite Hierotheos S. Vlachos

A'
Illustrations

1. The Creation

1. God created the whole world in five days.

2. On the sixth day He created man.

3. He placed him in Paradise.

2. The fall of man

4. Adam and Eve disobeyed God's command
and ate the forbidden fruit.

5. They lost their communion with God.

6. They came out of Paradise.

7. The exile began.

ὁ Κάιν κ̣ ὁ Ἄβελ

8. Thus death came into their life.

3. The incarnation of the Word

9. The Son and Word of God became man.

10. Christ is God-man: He is perfect God
and perfect man.

11. Therefore He is the one and only Saviour of men.

12. He is a shepherd, physician, father, brother and friend

4. Christ's life and work

13. Christ was born of the Virgin Mary
as man in Bethlehem during the rule
of Caesar Augustus.

14. He lived in our own circumstances.

15. He taught the people.

16. He performed miracles.

17. He suffered and was crucified for man's salvation.

18. He rose, abolishing death.

19. He ascended into heaven.

20. He sent the Holy Spirit.

21. We see all these things in Holy Scripture.

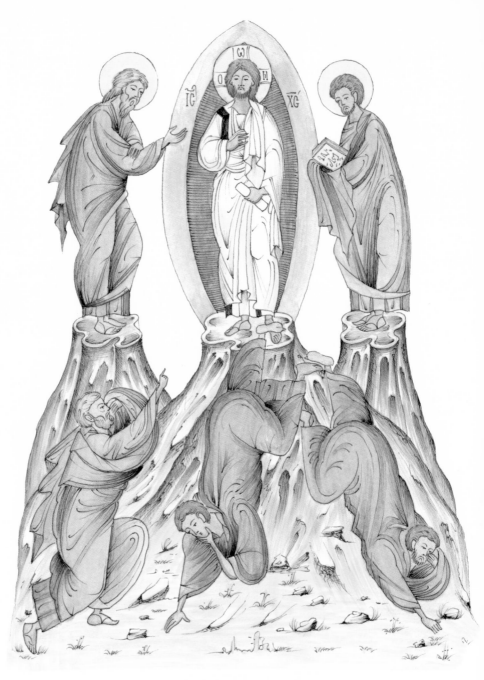

22. The Old Testament prophesies them,
the New Testament describes them.

5. The Triune God

23. Christ revealed to us that God is Triune:
Father, Son and Holy Spirit.

24. We do not understand this with our reason,
but it is a matter of revelation.

25. We live in the church, we keep Christ's
commandments and so we gain knowledge
of the Triune God from His energies, just as
we gain knowledge of the sun from its rays.

6. The Church

26. On the day of Pentecost the Holy Spirit descended and
the disciples became members of the Body of Christ.

27. Thus we have the Church as the Body of Christ.

28. There are many images to show what the Church is,
such as the shepherd, the Kingdom,
the wedding, the vine, etc.

29. The saints and all who live sacramentally and
wish to become saints belong to the Church.

30. It is only in the Church that we can be saved.

31. Outside the Orthodox Church there are heresies,
    as well as other religions.

32. There are three basic sacraments: Baptism, Chrismation and the Holy Eucharist.

33. In addition to these there are confession,
ordination, marriage and unction.

34. Through Baptism we reject Satan
and are united with Christ.

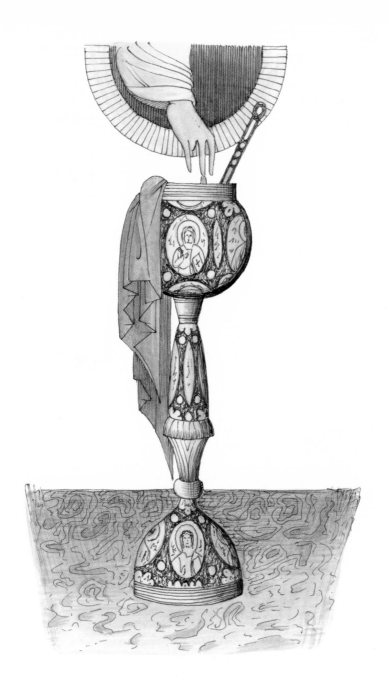

35. Through the Holy Eucharist we partake
    of the Body and Blood of Christ.

36. We should commune frequently,
after suitable preparation.

37. In the Divine Liturgy we experience communion
with Christ and our brothers.

38. The Orthodox Church includes the Patriarchates (Ecumenical, Alexandrian, Antiochan, Jerusalem, Russian, Serbian, Rumanian, Bulgarian), the Autocephalous and autonomous Churches, Dioceses and Parishes.

7. The holy Temple, a church

39. The place where the members of the Church
gather to worship God and to pray is called
a holy Temple, a church.

40. In a church many services and sacraments take place,
such as Vespers, Matins, the Divine Liturgy,
all the sacraments, parakleses, akathists.

41. There are many liturgical objects in the church.

42. The holy icons have great significance.

43. We should go to church often in order to have
    unity with Christ and our brethren.

8. The Orthodox Clergy

44. The Clergy are fathers, shepherds, physicians.

45. There are three degrees of priesthood:
Bishop, Priest and Deacon.

46. There are also other, lower church officials,
such as the reader, the cantor, the verger, etc.

47. Many people assist in the celebration of the
services and the administration of the church.

9. The Abolishing of Death

48. Death was abolished by Christ's Resurrection.

’Η ΚΟΙΜΗСΙС ΤΗС ΘΥ

49. What is called death today is a sleep.

50. The places where the bodies of those who have
fallen asleep are buried are called cemeteries.

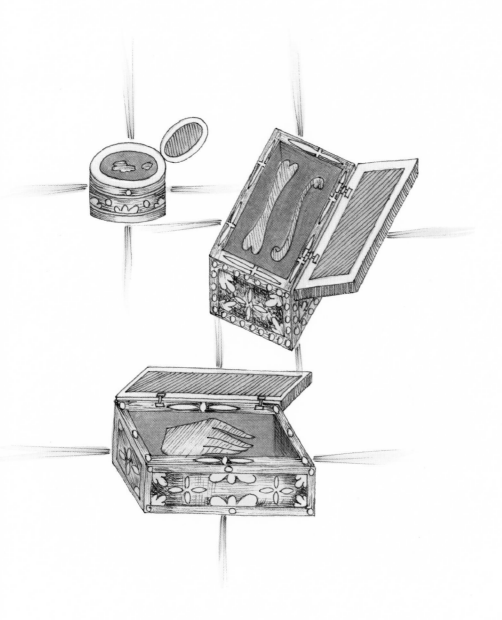

51. The holy relics of the saints are proof
that death has been abolished.

10. Resurrection of the dead and eternal life

52. Christ will come again to judge men.

53. This is called the Second Coming.

ΠΕΡΊ ΔΕ
ΤΗϹ ΗΜΈ
ΡΑϹ ἘΚΕΊ
ΗϹ ΚΑΊ ὭΡ
ΑϹ ΟΥΔΕΊϹ
ΟἸΔΕΗ.....
ΕἸ ΜΗ Ὁ
ΠΑΤΗΡ....

54. The day when He will come is not known.

55. Our bodies will be raised; that is to say
our souls will enter them, and there will be
a judgement, a tribunal.

56. After that, the Kingdom of God will begin
for the righteous, who even now are
enjoying it in part, as a pledge.

57. For the unrepentant there will be eternal Hell.

Conclusion

58. We live in the Orthodox Church, we keep God's
commandments, we take part in
the sacraments in order to live eternally
with the Triune God in His Kingdom.

B'
Brief explanations

1. The Creation

1. On the first day God created light.

On the second day He created the firmament and separated the heaven from the earth.

On the third day He separated the dry land from the sea and gave the command for the earth to produce growing things.

On the fourth day He commanded the sun, moon and stars to appear.

On the fifth day He created the fish of the sea and the birds of the sky.

On the sixth day He created the animals of the dry land, and man.

Before making the material creation He created the angels. Thus He first created the noetic world (angels), then the sensory world (the whole universe) and finally man, who is both noetic and sensory.

2. In the beginning He created Adam, and then from his rib He created Eve. Man is made up of a soul and a body. The soul did not exist before the body, nor the body before the soul, but the whole man was created at the same time. Man is the summing up of the entire creation, the microcosm within the macrocosm.

3. Paradise, in which man was placed right after his creation, was sensory and intelligible. It was sensory because it was a concrete place, and intelligible because man had the Grace of God. His unity with the Grace of God is seen from the fact that he was naked and did not feel his nakedness.

2. The fall of man

4. At his creation man was not perfect, but spiritually an infant. So it was necessary for him to reach perfection through a free testing, a voluntary struggle to attain perfection. This had to come about through obedience to God's command. Therefore God told him not to eat the fruit of one particular tree. The Fathers of the Church say that this tree was the vision of God, which men must not attain before being tested and prepared. But the first created human beings disobeyed God's command and ate of the forbidden fruit: they wanted to attain deification without obedience to God. Their disobedience was through the advice and instigation of the devil, who appeared as a serpent, and who had previously been an angel, but through pride became a devil and lost the Grace of God.

5. By disobeying God's command Adam and Eve lost divine Grace. In other words, they lost communion and unity with God, but they also lost communion with each other. The result of this sin was that death entered their life. The picture shows Adam and Eve separated from God and from one another. We also see that while they had previously been naked, they are now wearing garments of skin, the skins of animals. The teaching of the holy Fathers shows us the truth that the garments of

skin are decay and mortality. By decay and mortality
we mean illnesses, trials, afflictions and finally separation of the soul from the body.

6. When, after their sin, Adam and Eve lost their
communion with God, they came out of Paradise, that
real and blessed place.

7. This was the beginning of the period of exile, known
as Adam's lamentation. The hymns sung in the Church
on Cheese Fare Sunday describe Adam's lamentation at
losing the comfortable life of Paradise. The whole area
of our lives now is actually an exile, and we are struggling to get back to Paradise once more. In the funeral
service we sing: «And grant me the home country of
my heart's desire, making me again a citizen of Paradise». But even after the departure from Paradise God
continued to love and be concerned for man, and therefore He gave His Law, sent the Prophets, etc.

8. The fact that death had entered the life of Adam
and Eve was clearly shown for the first time when Cain
killed his brother, the righteous Abel. Then for the first
time Adam recognised the tragicalness of death.

3. The incarnation of the Word

9. Christ, the Second Person of the Holy Trinity,
through the good will of the Father and the cooperation
of the Holy Spirit, became incarnate. That is to say He
became man, assumed human nature, in order to save
man. He assumed mortal nature so as to conquer death's
power over it. Christ is not a philosopher, moralist, so-

cial reformer or leader of a religion: He is the conqueror of death.

10. We call Christ Godman because He is perfect God and perfect man. He had all the characteristics of human nature, without sin, but at the same time He was God. This union took place for the first and only time in the Person of Christ. Since He made human nature divine, we too have the possibility of being made divine. The fact that human nature is for ever united with the divine is salutary for us because we can receive the Body and Blood of Christ.

11. In this light we can see that Christ is the only saviour of man. No one else can free man from the tyranny of death, sin and the devil. In the picture we show that Christ saved the Samaritan woman and gave her what no one else could give.

12. Holy Scripture contains many images that point to Christ's work. Christ is a shepherd because just as a shepherd looks after his sheep and sacrifices himself for them, so does Christ. He is a physician because He cures men's sick souls. He is a father because he gives us rebirth into a new life and takes a personal interest in us. He is a brother and friend because he is very intimate with us.

4. Christ's life and work

13. The Gospels describe the events of Christ's incarnation. He was conceived in the womb of the Mother of God by the energy of the Holy Spirit, that is to say without the intervention of a man. He was born of the

Virgin Mary in a cave in Bethlehem. This event is supranatural but also historical, because it took place while Caesar Augustus was ruler of the Roman Empire. The angels sang praises at His birth, the shepherds were told about the event by an angel, the Wise Men from the east, guided by a star, came to worship Him.

14. Christ grew up within His family, helping Joseph the husband of His All-holy Mother, and showing obedience to them. At the age of twelve He went to the Temple and roused the interest of the Scribes and Pharisees, impressing them with the questions He asked. In general He lived within the conditions of our own life, since He was a perfect and complete man.

15. After His Baptism in the river Jordan His real work began. He taught the people, revealing what God is –that He is Triune Father, Son and Holy Spirit - what man is, what man's goal is, and how he should live on earth. We can see these revealing truths in the New Testament. The parables spoken by Christ are wonderful. Christ's words were comforting and saving.

16. The New Testament describes some of the miracles which Christ performed, curing various illnesses and giving new life to the people. The miracles were a confirmation of the fact that He is the Son of God, that He is the Messiah who was awaited by the Jews, as well as by all men.

17. Three years after He began His work He was arrested by the Jews because He said that He was the Son of God. He suffered greatly and was finally crucified at Golgotha. We are shown His Passion and cruci-

fixion very impressively both in the Gospels and in the services of Holy Week, especially those of Great Thursday and Good Friday. He was crucified for our sakes, in order to grant us life and to free us from the prison and tyranny of death.

18. On the third day after His death He rose from the dead and so destroyed the power of death. In the Orthodox Church the icon of the Resurrection shows Christ descending into Hell and saving the righteous men of the Old Testament. Christ did really descend into Hell, doing away with its power. This is depicted as the shattering of the gates and the breaking of the locks. The Resurrection is painted in this way because no one saw Christ at the moment when He came out of the tomb. There are also icons which show Him appearing to the myrrh-bearing women and to His disciples. Any way the icon of His descent into Hell indicates His victory over death. Therefore ever since that time the separation of every man's soul from his body has been called sleep.

19. Forty days after His Resurrection He was taken up into heaven, and thus He lifted deified human nature up to the throne of God, where He had always been as God. As He ascended into heaven He blessed His Disciples, and the angels gave them assurance that He would come down to earth in the same way to judge men at His Second Coming.

20. Ten days after His Ascension and fifty days in all after His Resurrection He sent the Holy Spirit, the third Person of the Holy Trinity, Who proceeds from the Father and is sent by the Son. The Disciples actually

saw the presence of the Holy Spirit resting in tongues of fire on their heads.

21. In Holy Scripture we encounter all the events of the creation of the world, the fall of man, and the incarnation of Christ. Holy Scripture consists of the 49 books of the Old Testament and the 27 books of the New Testament. We should study Holy Scripture in the life of the Church and the teaching of the holy Fathers.

22. Christ is the centre of Holy Scripture. The Old Testament prophesies and prepares for His coming, and the New Testament describes it and presents His work. This is well expressed in the event of Christ's Transfiguration. The Apostles are representatives of the New Testament and the two men who appeared, Moses and the Prophet Elijah, are representatives of the Old Testament.

5. The Triune God

23. One of the basic purposes of Christ's incarnation was to reveal that God is a Trinity: Father, Son and Holy Spirit. Christ revealed this truth to the Samaritan woman, among others, when He said: «God is Spirit, and those who worship Him must worship in spirit and truth». This means that God the Father is worshipped in the Holy Spirit and in Christ, who is truth. There is unity among the persons of the Holy Trinity. They have the same nature but different persons. One example which does not apply absolutely is the example of men. All men have the same nature, but they are different persons. In the Divine Liturgy we sing: «Father, Son, and Holy Spirit, consubstantial, undivided Trinity».

24. The great truth of the Triune God cannot be understood by human reason, but it is an object of revelation. When a man attains deification, vision of the uncreated Light, then he understands that God is Triune. The Disciples on Mount Tabor were transformed, and so they saw the divinity of the Word as Light, the Holy Spirit as a luminous cloud, and heard the voice of the Father.

25. For our part, we continue in the Church and receive the energies of the Triune God, and so we acquire knowledge of God. Therefore this is a matter of spiritual experience. Abraham's hospitality is a representation which points to the Triune God, Who not only has been revealed but also is experienced through Christ.

6. The Church

26. With the creation of the angels and men we have the first phase of the Church. Then through the fall of men we had the fall of the Church. Nevertheless a small remnant of the Church remained in the persons of the Prophets and the righteous men of the Old Testament. However, through the incarnation of Christ, and especially with the descent of the Holy Spirit on the day of Pentecost, the Apostles became members of the Body of Christ, members of the Church. Thus the Church of the Old Testament, which was spiritual, now became fleshly, the Body of Christ. The illustration we give combines Pentecost and Holy Communion, showing that the Church as the Body of Christ begins at Pentecost and is experienced in the holy Eucharist, which is the centre of the Church and makes it the Body of Christ.

27. The Church is not a human organization but a divine organism, it is not a corporation but the Body of Christ. Christ is the head of the Church and its members are the Christians who have been baptised and are conforming their lives to Christ.

28. There is no definition for the Church except that it is the Body of Christ. In Holy Scripture there are many images which show the nature of its work and its mission. The main image used by Christ is that of the vine. Christ is the vine, and the faithful are the grafts which are joined with Christ and receive all their strength from Him. Elsewhere the Church is called a flock, because it is led by Christ the true shepherd and is fed by Him. It is also characterised as a marriage, to show the unity of the faithful with Christ: Christ is the Bridegroom and the Church is the Bride. It is called a Kingdom because Christ is the eternal King and the Christians are His subjects who do His will.

29. The true members of the Church are the saints, that is to say the Prophets, Apostles, Martyrs, holy men and ascetics, and those who married and lived in the world and have fallen asleep in peace. In general the members of the Church are the deified, that is to say those who at different depths partake of the uncreated Grace of God. But those who are living sacramentally and, in imitation of the saints, are struggling to be cured are also members of the Church.

30. The Church is the ark of salvation. In away it resembles the Old Testament ark which saved Noah from the flood with his family and the various animals. All

who enter the Church and strive to keep God's commandments are saved.

31. The Orthodox Church has preserved the truth as Christ revealed it to us, as the holy Apostles handed it down and all the saints lived it. It is from this Orthodox Church that other Christians were separated and other Christian churches or confessions were formed. Two such large Christian «Churches» are the Papacy, which is so called because the Pope constitutes the authority, and Protestantism, which is divided into many off-shoots. Apart from the heresies, there are also other eastern religions, such as Hinduism - brahmanism - buddhism, Mohammedanism etc.

32. The Fathers teach that there are three basic sacraments in the Church. One is Baptism, which is called the introductory sacrament, for it is through this that we are brought into the Church. The second sacrament is chrismation, through which we receive the gifts of the Holy Spirit and which is linked with Baptism. And the third is Holy Communion. We are baptised in order that as members of the Church we may partake of the Body and Blood of Christ.

33. Since Baptism does not put an end to sin, we have the sacrament of repentance and confession, which is a second baptism, because it brings us back to the purity which we acquired through holy Baptism and makes us living members of the Church once more. We confess our errors to our spiritual father and receive healing. Another sacrament is that of ordination. Through ordination the apostolic Grace and blessing are transmitted to every generation. The Clergy are successors to the Apostles. It is they who celebrate the sacrament of Holy Communion, they who perform all the other sacraments and they who guide and cure the people of God. Through the sacrament of marriage the bridegroom is united with the bride, and they form the Christian family. There is also the sacrament of Holy Unction, by which our body is anointed with consecrated oil and we ask God to cure our soul and body.

34. Baptism is called the introductory sacrament, because through it we become members of the Church. In the sacrament of Baptism we renounce the devil, that is to say we free ourselves from the devil's power which works on us through our passions and desires, and we are united with Christ. Thus the image is purified and the person's nous is illuminated. We are brought back to the paradise which we left by committing sin.

35. The central sacrament of the Church is Holy Communion. All the other sacraments relate to this great sacrament. During the sacrament the priest asks the Father to send the Holy Spirit and transform the bread and wine into the Body and Blood of Christ. The Church cannot exist without the sacrament of Holy Communion.

36. The sacrament of Holy Communion is celebrated in order for us to partake of the Body and Blood of Christ. Christ said: «Unless you eat the flesh of the Son of Man and drink His blood, you have no life in you». Through Holy Communion we attain the true life which is Christ. Therefore we must commune frequently. How frequently depends on the spiritual condition of each person. This means that preparation is needed, which consists of repentance, confession, healing and prayer.

37. Holy Communion takes place in order for us to be able to partake of the Body and Blood of Christ. Therefore it is a communion of man with God. It is not a matter of sentiment or of a symbolic act. Through Holy Communion a person becomes «of one body and blood» with Christ. At the same time we attain communion with our brothers and feel them to be brothers of Christ and children of God the Father Himself.

38. The Church is one, because the Body of Christ is one. Since there are not many bodies there are also not many Churches. However, the one Church is articulated into partial Churches without the one Orthodox Church being broken. Of course we do not mean Papism and Protestantism, which we regard as confessions. So we have the Patriarchates and the Autocephalous Orthodox Churches. Each partial Church is articulated into Dioceses, and each of these into different Parishes, in order to serve better the needs of Christians. The unity of the Church is not broken by this subdividing, for each Diocese and each Parish is the whole Church in miniature. It is the same as with the bread, the Body of Christ, in the Liturgy. It is cut into pieces but not broken. Each Christian who receives communion does not receive one part of Christ's Body, but the whole Christ. The unity of all the partial Churches which compose the one Church is safeguarded by the same Faith (Orthodoxy), the same tradition, and their communion. This communion is expressed by mentioning the canonical Bishop. That is to say, in the Liturgy and in all the other sevices the priest mentions the canonical Bishop, the Bishop mentions his Archbishop, the Archbishop his Patriarch.

7. The holy Temple, called a church

39. The gathering and meeting of the members of a particular Church for the celebration of the Eucharist takes place in a particular venue which is called a holy Temple. Since it is in this holy place that the members of the Church meet and constitute the Church, it is also called a church. In the early Church there were «house churches» and during the persecutions there were the catacombs, and after the end of the persecutions the holy Temples were built.

40. All the sacraments are performed in the church, especially the sacrament of the Eucharist. In addition to the sacraments, all the other services too take place in the church, such as Matins, Vespers, Intercessions to the Virgin Mary, Salutations to the holy Mother of God. Each service has a special meaning and significance, and we should take part in them as regularly as we can.

41. Since the church is for liturgical use, there are many liturgical implements and objects, such as the Chalice, the Holy Gospel, the Cross, the censer, the vessel in which we boil the water which the priest pours into the Chalice, the lance, etc.

42. Predominating in the church are the holy icons. We find them in the icon-stand when we enter the church, on the iconostasis and in the whole area of the church. Thus there are the icons of the iconostasis, the processional icons and hagiographic icons on the walls. The Orthodox icon expresses the truth of man's deification, because it shows that the saints saw the uncreated Light (the halo) and that even their bodies were transfigured.

We kiss the holy icons, making the sign of the Cross out of reverence, but also to acknowledge that the saints experienced the Cross of Christ in their lives, and also because we acknowledge that we too will live this life of the Cross, that is to say we will keep Christ's commandments. When we kiss the holy icons, we are not kissing the wood or the material object of which it is made, but the person depicted; in other words, the honour goes to the prototype.

43. It is not enough for an Orthodox Christian to have been baptised, but he must live the sacramental life of the Church and pray to God and feel that he belongs to a community, to a family. He lives in this way when he goes to church regularly. Therefore we must continuously attend church, and especially receive Holy Communion every Sunday and every great feast. Thus we will come to feel that we are not alone and orphans but that we have a Father and brothers.

8. The Orthodox Clergy

44. Since the Orthodox Church is a family and a hospital which cures a person in order to bring him to unity with God, it means that the Clergy are the fathers of this family, that they are the shepherds of this spiritual flock which they are leading into green pastures, and they are the physicians who cure the wounded person. The Clergy are visible images of Christ. Just as Christ is a Father who begets us, a good shepherd, and a physician who cures us, so also the Clergy are fathers, shepherds and physicians.

45. There are three degrees of the priesthood: deacon, priest and bishop. The bishops are successors of the holy Apostles. They are in the full sense of the word the shepherds who lead the people, and they ordain the other Clergy. The priests are responsible for a Parish. With the blessing of the bishop they perform all the sacraments, excepting that of ordination. The deacons assist the bishop and the priest and they do not perform any sacrament. In order of ordination, a man is first ordained deacon, then priest and then bishop.

46. In addition to the three degrees of priesthood there are also other, lower Clergy. This category includes the reader, who reads the epistle and other texts, the cantor, who sings in the services on behalf of the people, the verger, who sees to the decorum of the holy Temple and the supply of things necessary for performing the sacraments, etc. These lower Clergy are appointed in a special service with a particular prayer which is read by the archpriest. This service is called the laying on of hands, while the sacrament for the three degrees of priesthood is called ordination.

47. For the good functioning of the Parish there are also other persons who assist the Clergy. Among these are the churchwardens, who are laymen who see to the management of the funds, the purchase of various objects, and the needs of one parish community. Likewise there is the fund for the relief of the poor, administered by various members who look after the benevolent needs of the Parish.

9. Abolishing of death

48. The most basic purpose of the incarnation of Christ is the abolishing of death. Through His Passion, Crucifixion and Resurrection Christ did actually do away with death. Death no longer has the power which it had in the Old Testament. Through Baptism and the Eucharist we are truly members of the Church, and we experience the abolishing of death, because we have become members of the risen Body of Christ and are in communion with His glorified and risen Body. That is to say, we are able to experience the abolishing of spiritual death, since we have been united with Christ and possess the assurance that our bodies will be raised at the Second Coming of Christ.

49. In the Orthodox Church death is called sleep, for after the separation of a man's soul from his body a man simply sleeps until the Second Coming of Christ. Sleep at night is a small death, and death is a great sleep. We see this very clearly at the time of the saints' departure from this world. They have an inner and outer calm, they are marked by a desire to meet Christ, and they possess the assurance that our bodies will rise again in the future. A characteristic feast is that of the Dormition of the Mother of God. The Church celebrates Christ's victory over death every Sunday and every feast day, because the day of every saint's death is glorious and his memory is celebrated then.

50. After the temporary departure of a person's soul from his body, the body is buried with reverence and care in a particular place which is not called a graveyard for the dead but a cemetery, a place of sleep, because the person is simply sleeping until the Second Coming of Christ. The Church has consecrated prayers for those who have fallen asleep, such as the funeral service, the memorial services, the thrice-holy hymns.

51. The holy relics of the saints, that is of the martyrs and ascetics are evidence that death has been abolished. The bodies of the saints are fragrant, they work miracles, and they do not decay. This shows that the saints are sleeping, that there is no death. All these things are explained by the fact that when the souls of the saints are separated from their bodies, divine Grace is not broken through but remains in both the soul and the body.

10. Resurrection of the dead and eternal life

52. It is the firm faith of the Church that Christ will come again to judge men, as He Himself disclosed. The fact that He will come again does not mean that He is not with us now, for He is the Head of the Church. It means to point out that He will come, our bodies will be raised, He will judge men, and the righteous will enter the Kingdom of God in soul and body.

53. The coming of Christ is called the second coming, as distinct from the first coming. The first coming, the incarnation, was humble, and in some way inglorious, for men did not recognise Him and they crucified Him. The Second Coming will be manifest and glorious since all will recognise Him and He will be accompanied by the angels.

54. We have the assurance that Christ will come, what-

ever happens, but we do not know exactly when that will be. Christ Himself said that the day and hour are not known. Christ will come suddenly when men do not expect Him. That is why we must always be ready.

55. The resurrection of bodies and the judgement of men are closely connected with the Second Coming of Christ. The souls will enter their bodies, the bodies will be raised from the tombs, people will possess spiritual bodies, because they will not need food, clothing, sleep, etc., and there will be a tribunal. People will be judged according to their works. In the icon of the Second Coming there is a scene which is called preparation of the throne. There is a throne, and on it is a book of the Gospel. This means that we will be judged on the basis of the Gospel, on the basis of Christ's commandments, according to how far we have kept Christ's commandments in our daily life.

56. After this tribunal the Reign of God will begin, which is nothing other than partaking of the deifying energy of God, communion and union with God, seeing and partaking of divine Grace. The righteous are already enjoying the Reign as a pledge, they have a foretaste of it after their soul leaves the body, and they will enjoy it eternally after the resurrection of their bodies as well, as in a marriage.

57. Those people who have not repented after committing sin and have not cured their souls, will not participate and commune with God, but will feel the caustic energy of God. This is called Hell, which will be eternal; that is to say it will never end.

Conclusion

We live in the Orthodox Church, we keep God's commandments, we receive the sacraments in order to live eternally with the Triune God in His Reign.

The Lord's Prayer

Our Father, who art in heaven,
Hallowed be thy Name;
thy kingdom come;
thy will be done, on earth as it is in heaven.
Give us this day our daily bread;
and forgive us our debts, as we forgive our debtors;
and lead us not into temptation, but deliver us from the
evil one.

(Matt. 6, 9-13)

The Beatitudes

Blessed are the poor in spirit, for theirs is the kingdom
of heaven.

Blessed are they that mourn, for they shall be comfort-
ed.

Blessed are the meek, for they shall inherit the earth.

Blessed are those who hunger and thirst after righteousness, for they shall be filled.

Blessed are the merciful, for they shall obtain mercy.

Blessed are the pure in heart, for they shall see God.

Blessed are the peacemakers, for they shall be called the
children of God.

Blessed are those who are persecuted for righteousness'
sake, for theirs is the kingdom of heaven.

Blessed are ye when men shall revile you and persecute
you, and say all manner of evil against you false-
ly, for my sake.

Rejoice and be exceeding glad, for great is your reward
in heaven.

(Matt. 5, 3-12)

The Ten Commandments

1. I am the Lord your God... you shall have no other gods besides me...

2. You must not make for yourself any carved image, or any likeness of anything in the heavens above, or on the earth below, or in the waters under the earth. You must not bow down to them nor serve them...

3. You must not take the name of the Lord your God in vain...

4. Remember to keep the sabbath day holy. Six days you must labour and do all your work, but the seventh day is the sabbath of the Lord your God...

5. Honour your father and your mother, so that you may enjoy long life in the land...

6. Do not commit adultery.

7. Do not steal.

8. Do not murder.

9. Do not bear false witness against your neighbour.

10. Do not covet... anything that is your neighbour's.

(Exodus 20, 1-17)

Other works by the same author

In English:

1. A night in the desert of the Holy Mountain, first edition 1991, reprinted 1994, second edition 1995, reprinted 1998, Birth of the Theotokos monastery, p. 200

2. The illness and cure of the soul in the Orthodox Tradition, first edition 1993, reprinted 1994, 1997 Birth of the Theotokos Monastery, p. 202

3. Orthodox Spirituality, first edition 1994, reprinted 1996, 1998, Birth of the Theotokos Monastery, p. 112

4. Orthodox Psychotherapy, first edition 1994, reprinted 1995, 1997, Birth of the Theotokos Monastery, p. 372

5. Life after death, first edition 1996, reprinted 1998, Birth of the Theotokos Monastery, p. 392

6. St. Gregory Palamas as a Hagiorite, Birth of the Theotokos Monastery, 1997, p. 400

7. The mind of the Orthodox Church, Birth of the Theotokos Monastery, 1998, p. 239

8. The person in the Orthodox Tradition, Birth of the Theotokos Monastery, 1999, p. 350

* * *

In Greek:

9. Mia vradia stin erimo tou agiou Orous, editions A'
   1978, B' 1979, Γ' 1982, Δ' 1984, E' 1985, ΣΤ' 1986,
   Z' 1987, H' 1989, Θ' 1990, I' 1992, IA' 1993, IB'
   1994, ΙΓ' 1995, ΙΔ' 1997, ΙΕ' 1998, Birth of the
   Theotokos Monastery

10. Osmi Gnoseos, editions "Tertios", Katerini 1985

11. Martiria zois, 1985

12. To Mistirion tis paedias tou Theou editions A' 1985,
    B' 1987, Γ' 1991, Δ' 1997, Birth of the Theotokos
    Monastery

13. Paraklitika, editions "Tertios", Katerini 1986

14. Orthodoxi Psychotherapia (Pateriki therapeutiki ago-
    gi) editions A' 1986, B' 1987, Γ' 1989, Δ' 1992, E'
    1995, ΣΤ' 1998, Birth of the Theotokos Monastery

15. Piotita zois, editions A' 1987, B' 1989, Γ' 1996, Birth
    of the Theotokos Monastery

16. Apokalipsi tou Theou, editions A' 1987, B' 1992, Γ'
    1996, Birth of the Theotokos Monastery

17. Therapeutiki agogi, editions A' 1987, B' 1989, Γ' 1993,
    Δ' 1998, Birth of the Theotokos Monastery

18. Sizitisis gia tin Orthodoxi Psychotherapia, editions A'
    1988, B' 1992, Γ' 1998, Birth of the Theotokos Mona-
    stery

19. Psychiki asthenia kai igia, editions A' 1989, B' 1991,
    Γ' 1995, Birth of the Theotokos Monastery

20. Anatolika I, editions A' 1989, B' 1993, Birth of the
    Theotokos Monastery

21. Keros tou piisai, Birth of the Theotokos Monastery, 1990

22. To politevma tou Stavrou, editions A' 1990, B' 1992, Birth of the Theotokos Monastery

23. Ecclesiastiko fronima, editions A' 1990, B' 1993, Birth of the Theotokos monastery

24. Prosopo kai Eleftheria, Birth of the Theotokos Monastery, 1991

25. O Vlepon, editions A' 1991, B' 1992, Birth of the Theotokos Monastery

26. Orthodoxos kai ditikos tropos zois, editions A' 1992, B' 1994, Birth of the Theotokos Monastery

27. Mikra isodos stin Orthodoxi pnevmatikotita, Athens 1992

28. O Agios Grigorios o Palamas os Agioritis, editions A' 1992, B' 1996, Birth of the Theotokos Monastery

29. Katichisi kai Baptisi ton enilikon, Athens 1993

30. Romeoi se Anatoli kai Disi, Birth of the Theotokos Monastery, 1993

31. Paremvasis stin sychroni kinonoia A', Birth of the Theotokos Monastery, 1994

32. Paremvasis stin sychroni kinonoia B', Birth of the Theotokos Monastery, 1994

33. AIDS, enas tropos zois, 1994

34. To prosopo stin Orthodoxi Paradosi, editions B' 1994, Γ' 1997, Birth of the Theotokos Monastery

35. Epoptiki Katichisi, editions A' 1994, B' 1999, Birth of the Theotokos Monastery

36. I zoi meta ton thanato, editions A' 1994, B' 1995, Γ' 1996, Δ' 1997, E' 1999, Birth of the Theotokos Monastery

37. I Despotikes eortes, editions A' 1995, B' 1999, Birth of the Theotokos Monastery

38. Iparxiaki psychologia kai Orthodoxi Psychotherapia, editions A' 1995, B' 1997, Birth of the Theotokos Monastery

39. Osoi pistoi, Birth of the Theotokos Monastery, 1996

40. Gennima kai thremma Romeoi, Birth of the Theotokos Monastery, 1996

41. Entefxis kai synentefxis, Birth of the Theotokos Monastery, 1997

42. Ikonofiliko kai Iconoclastiko pnevma, Birth of the Theotokos Monastery, 1998

43. Kosmima tis Ekklisias, Editions of the Birth of the Theotokos Monastery, 1999, p. 800

* * *

In other languages:

44. Entretiens avec un ermite de la Sainte Montagne sur la priere du coeur, Editions du Seuil, 27, rue Jacob, Paris VIe, p. 192

45. Conversationes con un ermitano del Monte Athos, Narcea, S.A. De Ediciones, 280 39 Madrid, p. 196

46. أمســـــية في برّيــــة الجبـــــل المقـّـس آثوس
حوار مع ناسك حول الصلاة   ١٩٨٦

47. ОДНА НОЧЬ В ПУСТЫНЕ СВЯТОЙ ГОРЫ, СВЯТО - ТРОИЦКАЯ СЕРГИЕВА ЛАВРА 1993

48. ПРАВОСЛАВNAЯ ДYХОВNОСТБ,
СВЯТО - ТРОИЦКАЯ СЕРГИЕВА ЛАВРА 1998

49. ВЕЧЕ У ПУСТИНЬИ СВЕТЕ ГОРЕ,
МАНАСТИР ХИЛАНДАР, СВЕТА ГОРА АТОНСКА 1995

50. Egy éjszaka a Szent Hegy sivatagában, VS Studio, Budapest, 1997

51. Bevezetés a keleti keresztény lelkiségbe, Ortodox lelkiség, zöld-S (vs) Studio, Budapest, 1998

52. O noapte în pustia Sfântului Munte, Editura ICOS, 1999, Cluj-Napoca, str. IULIU MANIU, Nr. 40, Ap. 5

* * *

53. Secularism in church, theology and pastoral care, "The truth", ἀϱ. φύλ. 11, 29 Μαΐου - 5 Ἰουνίου 1994, W. Australia and "Alive in Christ", the magazine of the Diocese of Eastern Pennsylvania, Orthodoxy Church in America, Volume X, No 1, 2, 1994, καί Divine ascent, a journal of Orthodox faith, exaltation of the Holy Cross 1997, Vol. 1, No. 2, p. 10-25

54. Die Autorität in der orthodoxen Kirche (Kurzfassung der Einführung für deutsche Theologiestudenten am 29.9.1996), εἰς Philia, Zeitschrift für wissenschaftliche, ökumenische und kulturelle Zusammenarbeit der Griechisch-Deutschen Initiative, II/1996.

55. СЕКУЛАРИЗАМ У ЦРКВИ, БОГОСЛОВЉУ И ПАСТИРСКОМ РАДУ, СВЕТИ ГОРА, τεῦχος 68, 69, 1998

56. ВОСКРЕСЕНИЕ ХРИСТОВО, Крым 1998

57. The Church as a therapeutic center: the therapy of the soul, Divine ascent, a journal of Orthodox Faith,

The Entry into Jerusalem 1999, Vol. 1, No 3, 4, p. 62-79

58. Book review: Monastic Wisdom - Letters of Elder Joseph, The Christian activist, a journal of Orthodox Opinion, Vol. 13, Winter / Spring 1999, p. 9-10

Bishop of Nafpaktos
Hierotheos

Orthodox Psychotherapy

The science of the Fathers

translated by
Esther Williams

Metropolitan of Nafpaktos
Hierotheos

Life after death

translated by
Esther Williams

Archim. Hierotheos Vlachos

The illness and cure
of the soul in the
Orthodox tradition

translated by
Effie Mavromichali

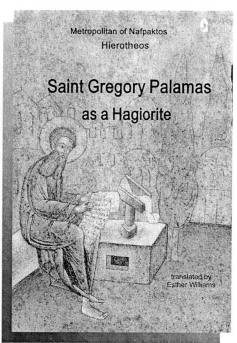

Metropolitan of Nafpaktos
Hierotheos

Saint Gregory Palamas

as a Hagiorite

translated by
Esther Williams

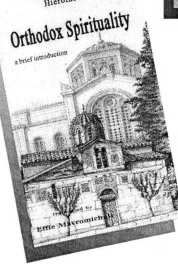

Bishop of Nafpaktos
Hierotheos

Orthodox Spirituality

a brief introduction

translated by
Effie Mavromichali

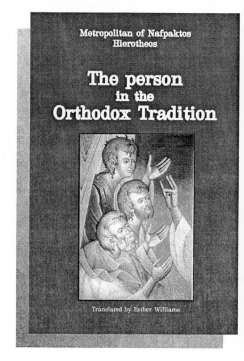

Metropolitan of Nafpaktos
Hierotheos

The person
in the
Orthodox Tradition

Translated by Esther Williams

Metropolitan of Nafpaktos
Hierotheos

The mind
of the Orthodox Church

Translated by
Esther Williams

In other languages

Hiérothée Vlachos
Entretiens
avec un ermite
de la sainte Montagne
sur la prière
du cœur

Seuil

narcea

ОДНА НОЧЬ
в пустыне
СВЯТОЙ ГОРЫ

Архимандрит Јеротеј Влахос

ВЕЧЕ У ПУСТИЊИ СВЕТЕ
ГОРЕ

КАРА МАЛЕКСАНДАР

Hierotheos Vlachos archimandrita

Egy éjszaka
a Szent Hegy sivatagában

Beszélgetés egy áthoszi remetével a Jézus-imáról

VS STUDIO

HIEROTEOS
Episcop de Nafpaktos

O noapte în pustia
Sfântului Munte

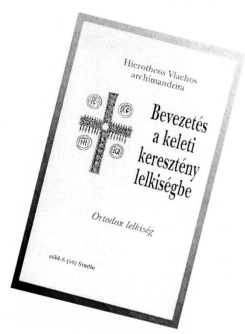

Hierotheos Vlachos
archimandrita

Bevezetés
a keleti
keresztény
lelkiségbe

Ortodox lelkiség

zöld-S (vS) Studio

These books can be found at:

the greek and english,
Birth of the Theotokos Monastery
GR-32100 LEVADIA, P.O. 107
GREECE
e-mail: pelagia@pelagia.org

the french,
Éditions du Seuil
27, rue Jacob, Paris VIᵉ

the spanish,
Narcea, S.A. De editionees,
Dr. Federico Rudio y Galí, 9. 28039 Madrid.

the arabic,
Archéveche Grec Orthodoxe
Beyrouth, Liban

the russian,
Свято- Троицкая Сергиева Лавра
Перевод с новогреческого
Художествнное оформление

the serbian,
Monastery of Chelandari
Mount Athos, Greece

the hungarian,
Zöld-S Stúdió (VS STUDIO)
1535 Budapest, Pf. 699

the romanian,
Editura ICOS
Cluj-Napoca, Str. IULIU MANIU, Nr. 40, Ap. 5
tel. 064-196.137